How Are Smartphones Made and Sold?

Derek Miller

Cavendish Square

New York

Published in 2020 by Cavendish Square Publishing, LLC
243 5th Avenue, Suite 136, New York, NY 10016

Copyright © 2020 by Cavendish Square Publishing, LLC

First Edition

Website: cavendishsq.com

This publication represents the opinions and views of the author based on his or her personal experience, knowledge, and research. The information in this book serves as a general guide only. The author and publisher have used their best efforts in preparing this book and disclaim liability rising directly or indirectly from the use and application of this book.

All websites were available and accurate when this book was sent to press.

Library of Congress Cataloging-in-Publication Data

Names: Miller, Derek L., author.
Title: How are smartphones made and sold? / Derek Miller.
Description: First edition. | New York, NY : Cavendish Square Publishing, LLC, [2020] | Series: Where do goods come from? | Includes bibliographical references and index.
Identifiers: LCCN 2019011207 (print) | LCCN 2019013606 (ebook) | ISBN 9781502650313 (ebook) | ISBN 9781502650306 (library bound) | ISBN 9781502650283 (pbk.) | ISBN 9781502650290 (6 pack)
Subjects: LCSH: Smartphones--Design and construction--Juvenile literature. | Cell phone equipment industry--Juvenile literature.
Classification: LCC TK6564.4.C45 (ebook) | LCC TK6564.4.C45 M55 2020 (print) | DDC 621.3845/6--dc23
LC record available at https://lccn.loc.gov/2019011207

Editor: Caitlyn Miller
Copy Editor: Denise Larrabee
Associate Art Director: Alan Sliwinski
Designer: Christina Shults
Production Coordinator: Karol Szymczuk
Photo Research: J8 Media

The photographs in this book are used by permission and through the courtesy of:
Cover, Asharkyu/Shutterstock.com; p. 5 TimeStopper/Moment/Getty Images; p. 7 onthewaybackhome/Shutterstock.com; p. 8 AarreRinne/E+/Getty Images; p. 11 Chris McGrath/Getty Images; p.12 Pe3k/Shutterstock.com; p. 14 Tomohiro Ohsumi/Bloomberg/Getty Images; p. 16 Pressmaster/Shutterstock.com; p. 21 Xiaolu Chu/Getty Images; p. 25 Colin Anderson Productions pty lt/DigitalVision/Getty Images; p. 26 Golubovy/Shutterstock.com; p. 28 Ollyy/Shutterstock.com.

Printed in the United States of America

Table of Contents

Chapter 1

Sourcing Smartphones

Smartphones connect people around the world. People send text messages with smartphones. People play games together with smartphones too. Making smartphones also connects people around the world. People need to work together to make them. Making and selling smartphones takes many steps. The first step is finding materials.

Basic Materials

Different materials are used to make smartphones. Glass, plastic, and metal are common materials.

Smartphones are made from many parts. These parts are made of different materials.

The screen is made out of glass. This glass is special. It needs to be thin so the touch screen works. Most smartphones use Gorilla Glass. It is

DID YOU KNOW?

The backs of smartphones are plastic, metal, or glass. Plastic is cheap. Metal is strong, and glass looks glossy.

glass made just for smartphones and tablets. It is strong and thin.

Smartphones also have plastic in them. Some smartphones have a plastic back. Other smartphones just have plastic inside of them.

Metals

Smartphones are made of different metals. Sometimes the back of a smartphone is metal. There is always metal on the inside. Electricity moves through metal wires in smartphones. Metal is used to make the chips in smartphones. Chips are

DID YOU KNOW?

Smartphones contain gold. Gold is used to make wires. One smartphone contains as much gold as 53 pounds (24 kilograms) of gold ore!

Ore is heated to obtain metal.

what make smartphones "smart." They are similar to chips used in computers.

Metals come from mining ores. An ore is rock that is part metal. The ore is taken out of the ground. The ore is **refined** to make pure metal from it.

Mining has some downsides. It creates pollution. Pollution is bad for the environment. Mining can

Mining can hurt the planet and cause conflicts.

make water unhealthy to drink. It can make air unhealthy to breathe.

In some countries, mining leads to fighting. People fight over mining because it makes money. Some ores are fought over. They are called conflict minerals. Smartphone makers need these minerals to make smartphones. They need to choose their materials carefully.

Rare Earth Elements

Rare earth elements are part of smartphones. Rare earths are seventeen different elements. They have strange names like "holmium." Small amounts of rare earths are needed for many different parts of smartphones.

Rare earths are not really rare. They are in dirt and rocks all over the world in small amounts. It is just expensive to get pure rare earths from the dirt and rock. Mining rare earths can also create pollution.

China produces most of the world's rare earths. Other countries could produce rare earths, but they do not want the pollution. Other kinds of mining in China leave a lot of dirt waste. This waste sometimes contains rare earths.

Chapter 2

Making Smartphones

Smartphones are made up of **hardware** and **software**. Hardware is the part that you hold in your hand. The screen, case, and parts inside are all hardware. Software includes the programs on the smartphones. Applications, or apps, and games are software. Without software, a smartphone would not be able to do anything.

Software

Workers called software developers make software. **Developing** software is the process of

Workers make smartphone hardware at factories, like this one in Turkey.

creating and testing software. Software developers work by writing code. Code is a set of instructions. The smartphone follows these instructions, and the software works.

The operating system is the most important software. It manages all the smartphone apps. Android is the most popular operating system (OS)

The Android operating system (OS) is the world's most popular OS.

for smartphones. Apple's iOS is the second most popular operating system. Apps are developed to work on one or both operating systems.

Testing

Operating systems and apps need to be tested. Testing makes sure that they are working properly. Developers and software testers look for errors called bugs. If they find any, they fix them.

DID YOU KNOW?

Samsung makes more smartphones than any other company. The Chinese company Huawei ranks second, and Apple comes in third.

The hardware is tested too. Smartphones need to work well and not break. Machines drop and twist a new smartphone. Hopefully, the smartphone doesn't break. If a model is too fragile, engineers try to make it better.

Hardware

Making the smartphone hardware is very difficult. First, the **components** are made. Components are small parts that go into the finished product. A smartphone camera is one component. The screen is another.

Materials from all over the world are brought to different factories. Factories usually **manufacture** just one component. Manufacturing is making something on a large scale. Factories can manufacture thousands of components every day.

Here, a factory worker makes camera lenses for smartphones.

One factory makes the screen. Another one makes the camera. A third makes the chips. There are many more components inside smartphones. Each factory has special machines to make one type of component. They also have people who specialize in working with that component.

A Finished Smartphone

After the components are manufactured, they are sent to one place. This is called the **assembly** plant. Machines assemble the smartphone. The components were made to fit together perfectly.

Most smartphones are assembled in Asia. China is the leading country in smartphone assembly. China even assembles smartphones for companies not based in China. Apple is based in the United States, and Samsung is based in Korea. They both assemble many of their smartphones in China.

China and some other Asian countries keep costs low. Many components are made there, so the components don't need to be moved very far. Labor is also cheap. Labor is work done by human beings, such as operating a machine in a factory.

Companies save money when labor is cheap because they don't need to pay workers much.

Human Capital

Different workers have different human capital. Human capital is how much money a person's labor is worth. Special skills increase a person's human capital. Software developers have high human capital. They are in great demand. Companies often pay them a lot of money.

Software developers have special skills. They can earn a lot of money!

Workers who assemble smartphones have less specialized skills. It is not easy to assemble a smartphone, but people can learn quickly. Learning software development takes years.

Intellectual Property Rights

The technology—the hardware and software—that goes into making a smartphone is very expensive. Smartphone companies closely guard their secrets. Companies that make components also protect their designs. They don't want other companies copying them. An idea that is protected from other people is called intellectual property.

It is illegal to steal another person's or company's intellectual property. Still, companies sometimes do take each other's ideas. Smartphone companies often take each other to court over this. They say a company stole their idea, software, or hardware. It is up to judges to decide if it is true.

Chapter 3

Selling Smartphones

Competition to sell smartphones is fierce. Most Americans own a smartphone. Companies do not need to convince people to buy a smartphone. They need to convince people to buy *their* smartphone.

Advertising

Smartphone companies usually advertise the features of their smartphones. High-quality cameras, screens, and audio are highlighted in commercials. Companies like Apple and Samsung also focus on their brand. They try to build an image of a quality company that people trust.

Smartphone companies sell different models of phones. Each company has a flagship phone. Flagship phones come with the best features. Companies show off their best technology with these phones. Flagship phones also come with a high price tag. They can cost $1,000!

Not everyone wants to spend so much on a smartphone. That's why companies also make midrange and budget smartphones. Budget smartphones can cost about $200. They don't

DID YOU KNOW?

There are about 800 million smartphone owners in China. That is more than any other country. The entire population of the United States is only 325 million people.

have all the features of flagship phones, but budget phones still work well. Midrange smartphones fall between budget and flagship models.

Sales

Once smartphones are assembled, they need to get to stores. For a good to reach the United States from Asia, there are two options. It can be transported by air or by sea. Ships are slow but cheap. Air shipping is expensive but fast. Most smartphones are shipped through the air. Companies need to get their new smartphones to stores quickly. This helps them compete with each other.

Smartphones are sold in different places around the world. Some stores just sell smartphones. People can compare all the different models.

Huawei is very popular in countries that sell phones this way.

In the United States, **carrier** stores are popular. Carrier stores are run by phone networks like Verizon, AT&T, and T Mobile. These companies sell plans that let people use smartphones. Most Americans buy their

Huawei phones are very popular in countries like Germany and Colombia.

smartphone from their carrier. This is very different from the rest of the world. This difference means that Huawei is not very popular in the United States. Carrier stores usually do not sell Huawei phones. They have deals with other smartphone companies instead.

A World Market

Smartphone companies ship their products to countries around the world. The three countries with the most people are China, India, and the United States. These three countries are also the top three markets for smartphones. Smartphone companies try to sell in these markets. They also look for new opportunities.

People in some places are buying more and more smartphones. In Africa and South America, more people use smartphones every year. This growth is helping smartphone companies make profits. As

DID YOU KNOW?

Smartphones have become very popular very quickly. In 2011, just one-third of Americans owned a smartphone. In 2019, eight out of ten Americans owned a smartphone.

more people buy their first smartphone, companies can sell more.

Software Updates

Smartphone software also needs to be put on phones. New smartphones are sold with an operating system and apps. When the software is updated, the smartphone downloads that update.

Downloading can take place using Wi-Fi. Smartphones can connect to Wi-Fi at homes and businesses. This is free for the smartphone user. Downloading can also take place using data. Data is sold by carriers like Verizon. Data costs money, but it is convenient because not all places have Wi-Fi.

Smartphone users can download new software on their phones. They can go to the app store and find games or useful tools. Some apps are free, and some cost money.

Chapter 4

Global Connections

People from around the world work together to make smartphones. Engineers work on a single component. Developers make the software. The smartphone is assembled in a factory and sent to different countries.

Working Together and Competing

Making a smartphone is a team effort. Companies must collaborate. "Collaborating" means working together. The smartphone designer needs to talk to the companies that make components. All the components need to fit together like a puzzle.

Smartphone companies also compete with one another. They all want to sell more smartphones. When they see a hit phone, they change their designs. For example, metal cases used to be the most popular. Soon, everyone made metal phone cases. Then, glass cases became popular. Soon, everyone made glass phone cases.

Some teams who design smartphones work in different places. They collaborate online.

New Ideas

In the future, smartphones will change. They will get faster and faster. They will be able to do more things

Smartphones that can fold are just one exciting new design.

at once. The phone network is also getting faster. Networks are being upgraded to 5G. 5G is much faster than 4G or 3G. Faster networks mean web pages and videos load quicker.

DID YOU KNOW?

Smartphones communicate by sending signals to cell towers. This is how smartphones send and receive data.

Smartphone features will also change. Companies are working on new features all the time. In the near future, many companies hope to manufacture foldable smartphones. Users will be able to fold the phone, and the screen will bend. This feature will allow for bigger screens that can still fit in a person's pocket.

Connecting the World

Smartphones connect people around the world. People use them to talk and text. With a click of a button, people can contact their friends and family. Smartphones help us stay in touch.

Smartphones also spread ideas. Talking to people far away can help everyone. People share their different ways of thinking about the world. Smartphones are helping the world grow smaller.

Smartphones help people stay in touch, even from far away.

Using smartphones brings people from faraway places together. Making and selling them does too.

DID YOU KNOW?

New high-end smartphones are intelligent. They can learn to recognize faces and places. In the future, their ability to learn will increase.

Glossary

assembly The putting together of all the parts of something.

carrier A company that runs a phone network, such as Verizon or AT&T.

components The parts of a machine or electronic device.

developing Designing, making, and testing something like software.

hardware The parts of an electronic device you can touch—not the apps or programs.

manufacture To make something in large numbers.

refined Made pure.

software The apps and programs on a smartphone or other electronic device.

Find Out More

Book

Greathead, Helen. *My Smartphone and Other Digital Accessories*. Well Made, Fair Trade. New York, NY: Crabtree Publishing, 2016.

Websites

How Smartphones Work

https://electronics.howstuffworks.com/smartphone1.htm

HowStuffWorks examines how smartphones work in six slides.

Software

https://www.bbc.com/bitesize/guides/zcxgr82

The BBC presents information about how software works.

Index

About the Author

Derek Miller is an educator from Salisbury, Maryland. He loves learning how objects we use every day are engineered. He also loves sharing that knowledge with students. His other books include *How Is Gasoline Made and Sold?*